History of Computers

In the mid-1900s, engineers created the first electronic computers. Early computers were huge, expensive machines that were created to solve math and science problems. Before computers, people solved these problems by hand. Scientists wanted technology that could work faster than humans. So, computing

Searching the internet has become a part of everyday life for most people.

Connecting to the Internet

In order to do an online search, a person has to be able to access the internet. Scientists created the internet in 1969. The name *internet* comes from the words *interconnected network*. Connected computers are a part of a network, and the internet connects networks. In other words, the internet is a network of networks. Routers are devices that help pass information along these networks. When a message goes from one computer to another, routers help it get to the right place.

Early computers took up whole rooms and were not useful for most people.

machines were invented to replace these human workers. Some computers were the size of whole rooms. They could quickly calculate numbers and decipher codes.

Programming is the process of giving computers instructions. Early computers were difficult to program. This meant they were only useful for a handful of experts. Only the US government, large companies, and universities used computers. Computer technology later improved. Computers became smaller and cheaper. They also evolved to do other tasks. Scientists created new programming languages that were more like the way people write. These new programming languages made it easier for more people to learn to program.

With programming, computers can be instructed to do many things. They can connect to local networks. They can run programs like games. Or they can access large collections of information called

DID YOU KNOW?

During World War II (1939–1945), the Allies created a computer to decipher codes. It helped reveal secret Axis messages.

DID YOU KNOW?

Arthur Samuel was a computer programmer. In the 1950s, he used the IBM 701 computer to design a program to play checkers.

databases. College students began to learn about computer programming in the 1950s. They used the IBM 650 computer. The IBM 650 was the first mass-produced computer. Still, only 450 of them were sold in its first year.

One major advancement that made computers easier to use was the keyboard. Before keyboards, people put punched cards into a computer. The computer read the pattern of punches to know what to do. In 1956, researchers at the Massachusetts Institute of Technology (MIT) experimented with direct input. They connected a typewriter electronically to a computer. This change made controlling a computer less expensive and easier. Now, even more people could program and use computers.

The 1973 Xerox Alto was one of the earliest computers with a screen. It resembles what people think of today as a desktop computer. The user could see icons and windows on the screen. They could connect to local networks. And they used a mouse to move a cursor around the screen and click icons. The Xerox Alto

The Xerox Alto was one of the first computers that looked like a modern computer.

inspired later computers, such as Apple's Macintosh.

As computers continued to advance, computer networks connected more people. Government offices and universities created huge amounts of data. The worldwide network became known as the internet. On the internet, people could access vast amounts of information. But to make that information useful, there would need to be a way to quickly search through it.

Computer technology developed in the 1970s and 1980s. Companies introduced the first personal computers. These were small and cheap enough for many people to buy. In 1977, Apple sold the Apple II. It included a keyboard, a case, and a cassette tape with a game, and it could connect to a television set. Millions of Apple II computers were sold. Later, Apple's Macintosh computer as well as IBM's PC (personal computer) became popular. Soon, personal computers could be found in millions of American homes. By the early 1990s, many people were beginning to connect to the internet at home. In those days, online search technology had not quite caught up to computer technology, however.

History of Search

As computers developed in the mid-1900s, scientists also studied ways to store vast amounts of information and search

through it quickly. In 1945, inventor Vannevar Bush noticed a dilemma. He knew a lot of information was being published, but there was no good way to access it. He wanted scientists to create a body of knowledge for everyone to use. He said, "Publication has been extended far beyond our present ability to make real use of the record." Bush said that

Vannevar Bush's ideas helped advance computer science.

even though people were making new discoveries faster than ever before, search technology had not changed for hundreds of years.

Bush's goal was to create a system that worked by association instead of by rigid **indexing**. Indexing means sorting items in a distinct order. For example, libraries use index systems to sort books in a logical and predetermined order. On the other hand, the human mind works by association. It does not sort items in any certain order. It realizes connections between ideas. Such associations can change over time and be different for different people. Bush thought computers should act more like human brains. Then they could find the information people wanted more quickly and easily. Bush's idea was revolutionary, but it was many years before scientists created something like it.

The father of modern search technology is Gerard Salton. During the 1960s, he worked with teams at Harvard University and Cornell University to develop the System for the Manipulation and Retrieval of Texts (SMART). SMART made it easier for someone using a computer to find information. It helped users sort through large databases. SMART used simple rules for searching. One type of search it could do was based on term frequency. Term frequency simply measures how often a specific word appears in a document.

For example, the term *penguin* is likely to appear more often in an article on Antarctica than in one about the Amazon rain forest. Term frequency was simple, but it was effective. It helped people find better results based on the keywords they searched. It led to the development of search engines.

The Web and Search Engines

Online searching is done on the internet. There are many networks across the world, and the internet connects them. Usually, people access the internet through the **World Wide Web**. The Web is a system that helps people get to the information

The internet is made up of a large collection of websites, such as Wikipedia. Each website is made up of at least one web page.

that is stored in networks. It is made up of a huge collection of web pages, which can contain text, pictures, and other kinds of information. Web pages are connected by **links**, chunks of text that the user can click to travel to a related page. Users can

As the internet grew, search engines needed to improve from the earliest forms of online searches to the efficient searches that people rely on today.

get on the Web using a program called a web browser.

When people talk about online searching, they are usually talking about searching the Web. There are many reasons someone might search online. They could be looking for a specific piece of information. Many use searches while they are studying. Some people search the internet for the answer to a question. Online searching has evolved over time.

People begin an online search with a search engine. A search engine is a computer program that users access through a web browser. It takes in one or more search words from the user. Then, it presents the user with a list of results that it found. Without search engines, it would be impossible to find the right information.

One of the first search engines was called the Archie Query Form, or Archie. It was created in 1990 by Alan Emtage.

Search Engines Today

One of the first search engines was Archie. It was simple and sorted through less information than search engines today. Now, there are many different search engines on the internet. Some popular search engines include Google, Yahoo!, and Bing. Each one organizes information slightly differently. People prefer different search engines for this reason. Google's search engine officially launched in 1998, and it has been popular ever since. In July 2018, Google searches made up more than 86 percent of all online searches on desktop computers. Bing (7 percent) and Yahoo! (3 percent) were used second and third most for searches, respectively.

Archie was created to solve the problem of scattered and unorganized data. It logged all the information on pages in a database. Each page had its own entry in the database. Having more entries allowed users to go directly to the page they needed. It used a system similar to SMART, matching search terms with items in this database. This helped people find what they needed. There were only 130 websites in 1993, but it was still important to be able to sort through them. By 2018, there were well over 1 billion websites. Online search technology has had to advance rapidly to keep up.

CHAPTER 2

The Evolution of Online Search

At first, online search was very limited. This was because search engine databases did not have many entries. In 1994, Brian Pinkerton created WebCrawler. It was one of the first search engines to index all of the text on a web page. But it only indexed 25 websites. Other companies quickly followed this idea. As the Web became available to more people, online search became more important. People had access to an abundance of information, and they needed a way to sort through it. Multiple search engines were created. Each one used its own **algorithm** for processing online searches. An algorithm is a set of instructions that tells the computer what to do. Modern search engines are slightly different from each other because of the algorithms they use.

Algorithms create maps of **entities** and how they relate to one another. An example of an entity is an individual web page on a website. A specific news article on a newspaper's website is an entity. But it might be related to another web page, such as an encyclopedia article on the same topic. Each web page is a

```
1  #!/usr/bin/env p
2  import sys
3  import os
4  import simpleknn
5  from bigfile imp
6
7  if __name__ ==
8      trainCollect
9      nimages = 2
10     feature =
11     dim = 3
12
13     testCollect
14         = te
15
16     featureDir
```

Instructions for computers are written using specific sets of terms and formatting known as programming languages.

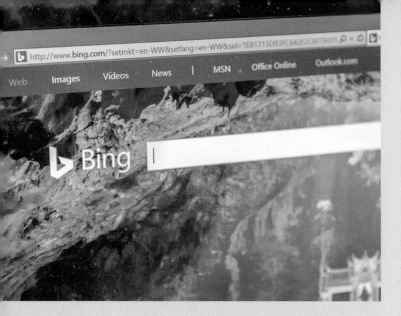

The search interface is how a user enters a query to perform an online search.

The algorithm is just one part of a search engine. There are several other important parts, too. They include the web crawler, the database, and the search interface. The web crawler is sometimes called a spider. It is a program that gathers information as it travels from link to link through the Web. It records what is on each page. It also records how pages link together. All this information is stored in the search engine's database. Finally, a person searching the Web uses the search interface. When the person enters a **query**, the search engine looks through

separate entity, and algorithms try to map the connections between entities. They can do this task in many ways. One way is to analyze the words and content on the page. Another way is to track links between web pages. A page that many other pages link to is seen as more popular. Tracking links is one way that Google's early algorithm worked.

the database to find relevant web pages. Then the search engine displays a search engine results page (SERP). The SERP is a list of web pages that the search engine's algorithm thinks are the best matches for the search term.

Challenges of Online Searching

In the early days of online search, there were many challenges. The goal was to find the right website. But it was not easy. After the Web became widely available, the number of web pages exploded. This made it even harder to find the right website. Search engine **indices** had too many entries. The designers of the search engines did not know how to organize these huge indices or make them easily accessible for people. Searching became

DID YOU KNOW?

One early search engine, AltaVista, helped bring important features to online search, including the use of natural language queries rather than specific keyword searches. Excite, another search engine of this time, offered many advanced search features.

frustrating for users. Someone had to use the exact wording of what they were looking for, or it might not come up on the SERP. It could take a long time to find the right information. Search engine developers wanted to provide reliable, informative results. That is why they focused on updating the algorithms to keep up with the growing Web.

Some of the main challenges were speed and order of results. Both the software and hardware related to online search had to evolve to get faster search results. The software needed algorithms that could organize lots of information. It needed to accomplish this not just quickly but also intelligently. A quick results page is not useful if the web pages

A SERP can bring up millions of results. How they are organized can make the difference in whether a user finds the correct information or not.

Paperwork

1-25 of 4,000,000+ results - Refin

One Stop Shop for **Online Deals**
Hot deals in 2009... You've come to
our **online** selection of top quality me
www.**online-deals**-from-us.com/deals
Cache

Online Deals that Can't Be Beat
Get the best online **deals** for whatever y
through so you'll be certain to make the b
www.class_act_**deals**_today/hot-products
webproducts_**online**.asp
Cache

Deal Hunter - Find Great **Deals Online** - D
Need help finding that perfect **deal**. You've co
online deal without any of the fuss that usua
www.**deal**-chaser-today-usamerica.net/proc
Cache

are not relevant to the user's search. Computers needed to be faster to be able to handle the amount of information the searches organized. Through the 1990s and early 2000s, engineers continued to make computers smaller and faster. Programmers improved algorithms to find good results more quickly.

Advanced Online Searching

Online search has evolved to predicting someone's search instead of just reacting to it. In 2008, Google introduced Google Suggest. It is an autocomplete feature. Its algorithm uses the letters and words in the search bar to predict what someone wants. It gives a dropdown list of predicted

BackRub

Google was originally known as BackRub. This is because the algorithm the search engine used looked at *back* links to understand how important a website was and what other sites might be related to it. Back links are clickable links on a web page that can send a user to the new page. The more pages that back link to a particular page, the more important and popular it might be.

In order to improve online searches, the hardware had to get better.

searches related to the keywords. This makes it easier for users to do an online search. It can save time typing out a long question, which also helps users search from smartphones with small keyboards. Many other search engines have added similar features. This is one example of how algorithms are continuously updated to make searching easier and faster.

Predictions, Not Suggestions

Despite the name of Google's original autocomplete feature, Google Suggest, the dropdown list of possible searches are predictions, not suggestions. Autocomplete is a part of Google's algorithm. It tries to predict what a person is searching for based on the letters or words in the search query. It also uses other information like the user's location and previous searches to predict the online search. The algorithm tries to help people find what they need.

CHAPTER 3

Online Search in Daily Life

Online search has become a part of daily life for many reasons. One reason is that devices that connect to the internet are now smaller. Computers used to fill rooms, but now they can fit in people's pockets. This makes them portable. In 1994, the term *smartphone* did not even exist yet. In that year, IBM created the Simon Personal Communicator. This device had features similar to smartphones today. It could send and receive emails, and it had a calendar, calculator, notepad, and more. The Simon would not fit in someone's pocket, but it was a mobile device. Other companies were working on small

DID YOU KNOW?

One Google search uses 1,000 computers to retrieve the information for the user.

computers and mobile phones, too. For many years, mobile phones lacked good web browsers. Few people did online searches on them.

That changed in 2007. In that year, Apple released the first iPhone. It had a touchscreen instead of a physical keypad. Users controlled the phone with their fingertips. It was different than other business-oriented smartphones. The iPhone made people want to use smartphones for more than business tasks. It was easy to use. Because of its powerful web browser, doing online searches from mobile devices became more popular. Since then, online searches on them have become routine. In 2018, half of all searches were made from mobile devices.

The Simon Personal Communicator integrated many functions that would later appear on smartphones.

Today, online search technology is at people's fingertips. It is easy to look up facts or answers to questions. Instead of waiting to ask the right person or going to

People turn to online searches for answers to many of their questions.

the library to find the right book, people can immediately find answers online. More than 84 percent of people turn to the internet when they want to find something out. People can also discover new information and ideas online. They can look at news stories, weather forecasts, dictionaries, and more. There is a vast amount of information on the internet.

Even with search engines sorting and ranking results, the vast amount of information and number of pages on the internet still leaves part of the evaluation to the user. Just because a page is a top search result does not mean that it is necessarily

Operating Systems

By the 2010s, the Apple iPhone had become an extremely popular device. It uses Apple's iOS **operating system**. The other major smartphone operating system is Android. It was created by Google. Apple's iOS only runs on phones made by Apple, but Google allows many phone makers to use Android on their phones. Samsung, HTC, LG, and other companies make phones that run Android. Because Google makes the Android OS (operating system), it integrates the Google search tools into Android phones.

the best, most credible, or most accurate for what the user is wanting to know. For academic information, users can often rely on university websites and peer-reviewed journal articles. Government websites are good sources of information. If someone wants to know what documents are needed to take a driver's exam, for example, the state's motor vehicle website is a more reliable source for that information than a personal blog post about the driver's exam.

Practical and Personal

Originally, the goal of online search was practicality. It was meant to help users find answers to queries. Personal

Search Engine Optimization

Search Engine Optimization (SEO) affects users' searches. Web pages that are optimized for how each search engine's algorithm works will be placed higher on the SERP. Web pages can be optimized for mobile or desktop searches for each engine. If a page loads quickly and is very readable on a phone screen, it will place higher on a SERP from a mobile phone. Web pages can also have tags that explain what the web page is about. This helps web crawlers sort them more accurately.

computers made online searches available to people, and they could find any kind of information by using search engines. Today, online search is not limited to one goal. It is intertwined with many other purposes. Online search has become much more than just practical. People can use it for fun, too.

Someone could use online search to find new games to download onto their computer. They could use it to look at the weather or shop for shoes. Every person can use it however they want. There are many reasons to search the internet. And with smartphones, online searches have become a part of daily life for many people.

Technology is advancing, and many devices are learning more about their users. Each time a person does a search, the search engine learns more about how the person uses it. Then, algorithms adjust future search results based on what it has learned. The device the person is using may also give information to the search engine. Some devices, such as smartphones, can detect where the user is. The algorithm may use this location information to improve results. For example, a user in New York who searches for "coffee shops" will get results nearby, rather than elsewhere in the country.

Privacy Concerns

Some people are worried about online privacy. They are concerned about how much data is collected and how it is used when they search. When someone searches the internet, search engine algorithms keep track of the information. Search engine companies make money by using that information to sell advertising to companies. Many advertising companies want the data gathered by search engines. It can tell them what people are searching for, who is searching for what company, and much more. The information helps

DID YOU KNOW?

Google performs more than 40,000 searches per second on average.

Google has expanded from a search engine company to include a marketing service that generates billions of dollars for the company.

companies design ads for more people and target the right people with the ads.

In 2018, Google made more than $109 billion, and most of that profit came from advertising. Google has two ad programs. AdSense is a program that website owners sign up for. They get paid based on how much their website users interact with the Google ads that appear on their website. So, the website owner can earn money by making space for ads on their website.

Google Ads is a program in which companies pay Google to display their ads. They pay per click, which means they pay when people interact with their ad. The amount of money a company invests, their keyword relevancy, and their overall brand quality determines where and when their ads are displayed. Companies pay to advertise with search engines because it allows their brand to be seen by more people. They want to be at the top of the SERP, so people will come to their website and become customers.

However, many people don't want search engines to record their search history or sell their personal information. DuckDuckGo is a search engine that was created in 2008. It was made for people who want to avoid all the data tracking. It protects people's privacy online because it does not record search history. On November 13, 2017, people made more than 20 million searches using DuckDuckGo in a single day. This shows that some people are concerned about privacy issues on the internet.

Because of users' privacy concerns, DuckDuckGo has found a market among online searchers.

DID YOU KNOW?

Google's parent company, Alphabet, earned $110.9 billion from ad revenue in 2017.

CHAPTER 4

The Future of Online Search

The future of online search is happening now. The internet changes and evolves every day. Search engine algorithms are updated. Social media accounts are created. News organizations track trends and important stories. Online search will continue to impact people as technology advances. And this impact will only grow as the technology continues to develop.

Companies have improved their online search results by getting to know people and using that information to update their algorithms. They want the user to have a good experience on the internet. Some examples of improvements include spelling corrections, faster results, search history, and search trends. When search engines keep track of what people search, they can help individuals find the

The internet grows and evolves every day as people use it.

At Facebook headquarters, an employee demonstrates how the search function integrates information from different places.

information they have searched for in the past. They can let people see trends about what other people are searching for across the world. These advancements have come a long way from original search engines' abilities.

Social media and other websites have evolved to allow online searches.

The search tool on Facebook allows users to search the internet and the Facebook network at the same time. If users were to search for a business, the results would include practical internet information, such as a street address. It would also show personalized information, such as Facebook posts about the business from family and friends.

Many people use online search to look at a wide range of results. Using a website's domain or Uniform Resource Locator (URL) is helpful for specific online searches. A website's domain is the name of a website. Youtube.com and wikipedia.org are examples of website domains. A URL is a complete web address that links to a specific web page.

The URL en.wikipedia.org/wiki/dog will take internet users directly to Wikipedia's page for dogs. Since a vast amount of information is available, narrowing search results by including a domain can be helpful.

DID YOU KNOW?

By using a pound sign or hashtag, social media users can mark that their post is about a certain topic. Users can search for related posts by using the same hashtag.

Conversational AI, such as Siri, can help people do more than look up information on the internet.

Computers That Talk

Artificial intelligence (AI) is changing the world of computers and online search. Programs with AI are designed to learn and make decisions on their own. Conversational AI technology is controlled by users speaking to it. When someone asks a question, the device senses the sound with a microphone. It analyzes the sound and figures out the words. Then it carries out a search to find the answer, and a computer-generated voice replies. All this happens within a few seconds.

Voice search and AI personal assistants are changing daily life for many people. Apple's voice-controlled assistant, Siri, is installed on iPhones. A person can ask Siri

AI and Internet Searches Moving to the Cloud

AI such as Siri, Google Assistant, and Alexa help make internet searches more natural. Users can simply ask Siri what the weather is like instead of typing out a search for the weather conditions for their location. Google Assistant can look up the time a store closes and automatically select the location closest to the user. Alexa can understand voice commands to play certain music or add items to an online shopping cart. AI's programming allows it to connect users to the internet in ways that were not previously possible.

to send a text message or find directions to a nearby business. In 2014, the online shopping company Amazon introduced its Alexa assistant. It can search the internet, create to-do lists, and play music. It also lets users buy things from Amazon using only voice commands. Google Assistant can find nearby restaurants and make a reservation. Microsoft's Cortana can pull up a SERP on a user's laptop or smartphone. Conversational AI can be connected to other technology. Speakers, computers, and smartphones are devices that commonly use it.

While conversational AI is impressive, it is not perfect. Some programs are great

Google Assistant is an example of conversational AI that is good at helping users navigate.

in one area but are not helpful with other tasks. Some conversational AIs are hard to set up. Some are great at providing directions but sometimes misunderstand what the users want.

The biggest benefit of conversational AI is that people can use it to search the internet in a natural way, which makes computers more accessible. For example, someone holding a crying

DID YOU KNOW?

An estimated 55.1 percent of the population of the world had internet access in 2018.

baby could search for soothing music to help the baby fall asleep, or a teenager who is texting a friend could ask what movies are playing at a nearby theater. Children or people who are unable to use a traditional computer can interact with conversational AI. All someone has to do is talk. Conversational AI keeps track of the things it talks about with people. It stores data in its memory and uses this information to provide better answers over time.

Many AI devices use **machine learning**. Machine learning is a science that aims for computers to learn on their own without additional programming. In 1954, Arthur Samuel experimented with machine learning in a checkers program.

Companies such as Amazon are hard at work trying to improve AI.

He played thousands of games of checkers against the computer, and over time, it learned how to play checkers better than Samuel. It played so many checkers games that it learned which moves would lead to wins and which would lead to losses. This is a simple example of how a machine learns to act when it has not been specifically programmed to do every action.

Google, Amazon, Microsoft, and Apple are all working on AI improvements. Instead of people asking AI devices questions, they want AI devices to be able to ask people questions. This would make the device more helpful. Predictive search technology means AI would anticipate someone's online search. For example, if someone opens a map application, or app, to get directions, the AI could suggest commonly visited addresses. It could predict that the person wanted to go to a location he has been to before. Or the AI could use information from another app to predict what the user wanted. If the calendar app had a doctor's appointment listed, the AI could predict that the person was going to her appointment. Predictive technology aims to make online search easier by decreasing the amount of time people spend searching or asking questions.

With machine learning, AI devices could become more like humans. They could take in data such as sound, visual, or text commands. Then they could process the data based on complex algorithms and memory. They could learn to think on their own and respond according to the situation. In 2018, many companies and scientists were working on new AI developments that could make online search even more powerful.

Future Technology

The future of online search will include more devices that connect to the internet. In the early days of the internet, only desktop computers went online. Later, laptops and smartphones began connecting to the internet. But today, many new kinds of devices are getting online. Personal assistant and AI devices can connect to the internet. They allow users to do online searches and get results.

The **Internet of Things** (IoT) is the connection of devices to the internet, especially nontraditional objects like cars or home appliances. When these objects are connected to the internet, they are called smart devices. The IoT is changing online search by making it more mobile and accessible than before. Someone driving a smart car could voice search. A person using a smart refrigerator could search for cooking videos. Researchers

DID YOU KNOW?

Smart devices such as watches make it easy to search the internet anywhere. People can ask about the weather before they go outside or find directions to a restaurant without having to use a normal computer.

Drag labels onto food items below
Remove
+ Day

Triple Fresh Cooling

3:21 AM

7 Days
2 Days

7 Days

milk

apples

People can now connect to the internet in new and interesting ways, including searching for recipes on a refrigerator.